The OXFORD *Essential* ATLAS

Acknowledgements

The publishers would like to thank the following
for permission to reproduce photographs :

Mike Dudley (with permission of NES Arnold) : 9
NRSC Ltd / Science Photo Library : 26
Tom Van Sant / Geosphere Project, Santa Monica,
Science Photo Library : 4, 5, 6, 7.

Cover image :
Tom Van Sant / Geosphere Project, Santa Monica,
Science Photo Library

Flag images :
© 1996 to the Flag Institute.
All rights reserved. .

The illustrations are by :
Bob Chapman
Carleton Watts
Jon Riley
Oxford Illustrators

The page design is by Adrian Smith

OXFORD
UNIVERSITY PRESS

Great Clearendon Street, Oxford Ox2 6DP

Oxford New York
Auckland Bangkok Buenos Aires Cape Town Chennai
Dar es Salaam Delhi Hong Kong Istanbul Karachi Kolkata
Kuala Lumpur Madrid Melbourne Mexico City Mumbai Nairobi
São Paulo Shanghai Singapore Taipei Tokyo Toronto

Oxford is a trade mark of Oxford University Press

First published 1997
Reprinted 1998, 1999, 2001, 2002

ISBN 0 19 831 841 3

Editorial Adviser

Patrick Wiegand

Oxford University Press

Contents

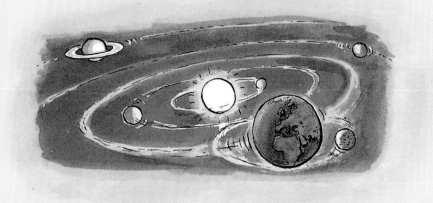

The Earth

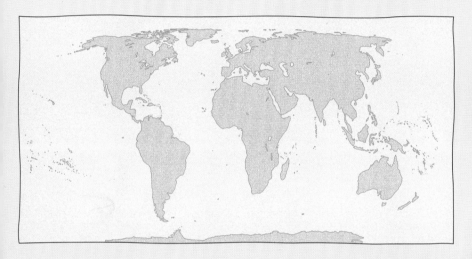

Maps of the World

Maps of Europe

2   A list of the maps in this atlas.

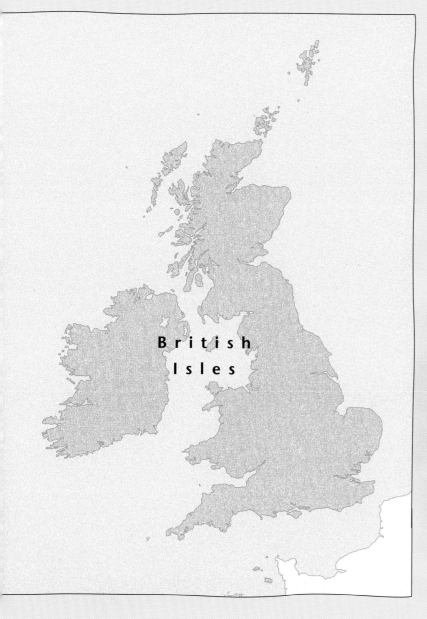

Maps of the British Isles

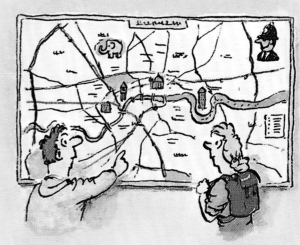

Index   page 32

4   This is the Earth in space.

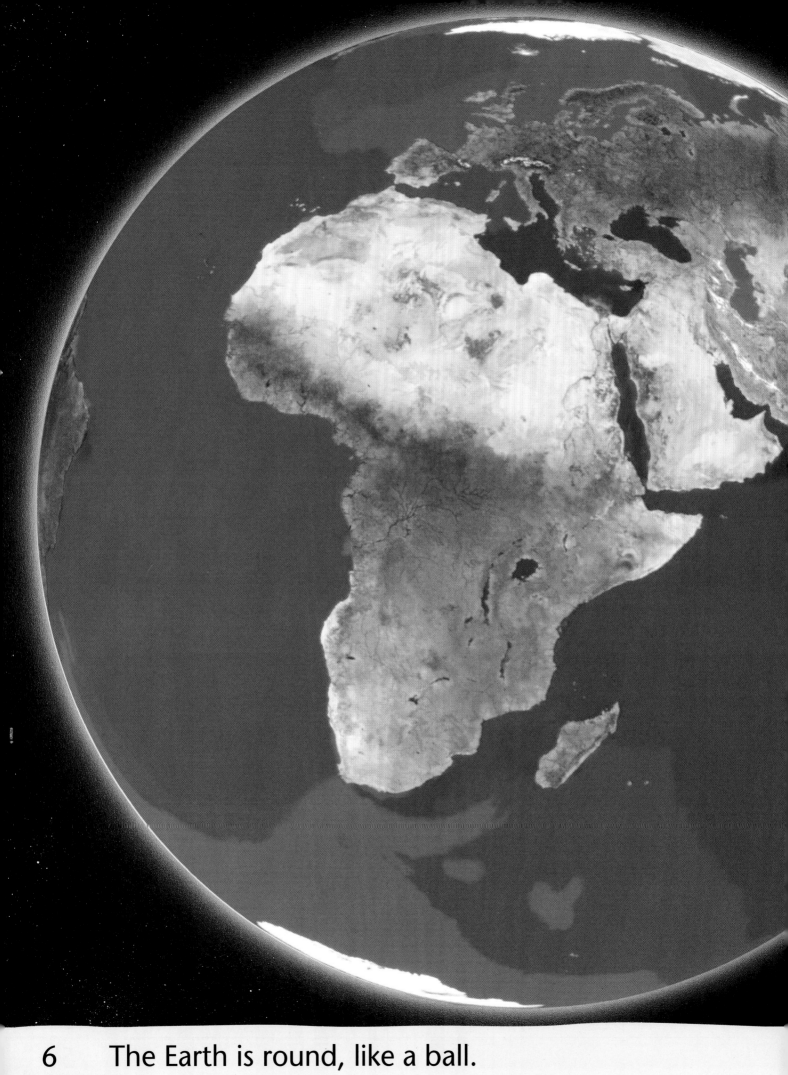

6   The Earth is round, like a ball.

8   There is land and sea.

A globe is a model of the Earth.

10   Each view of the Earth is different.

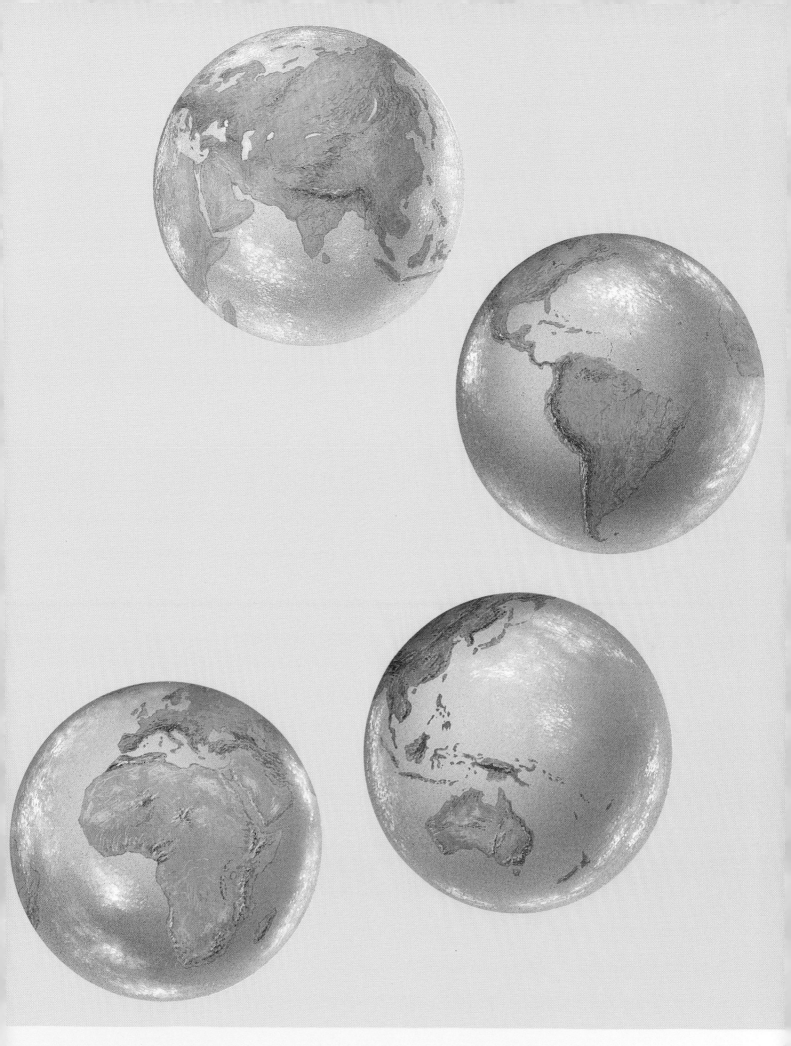

The World

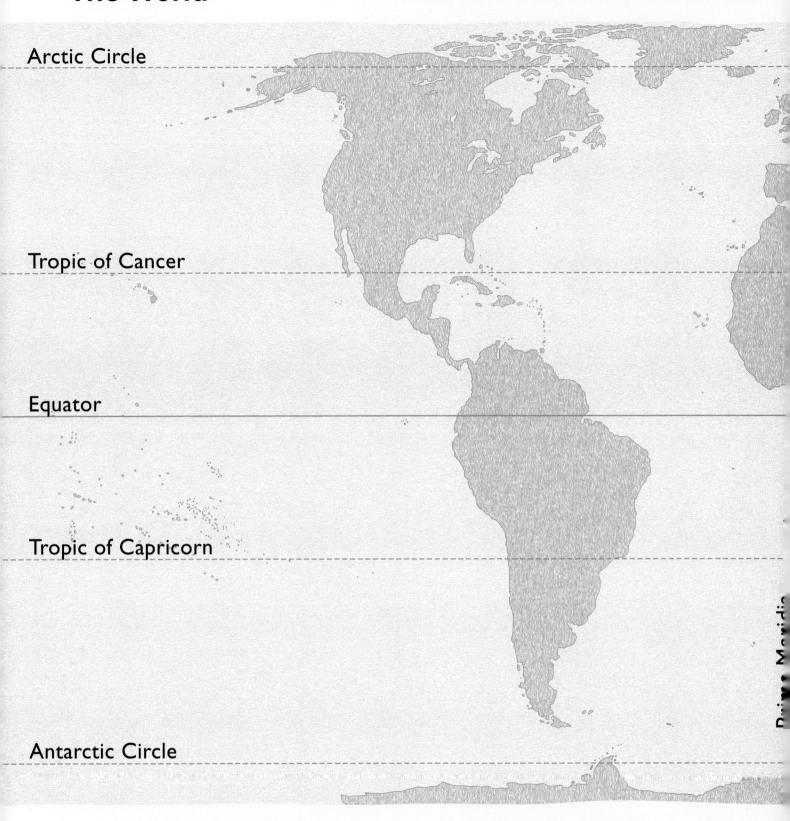

Arctic Circle

Tropic of Cancer

Equator

Tropic of Capricorn

Antarctic Circle

12   This is a map of the World.

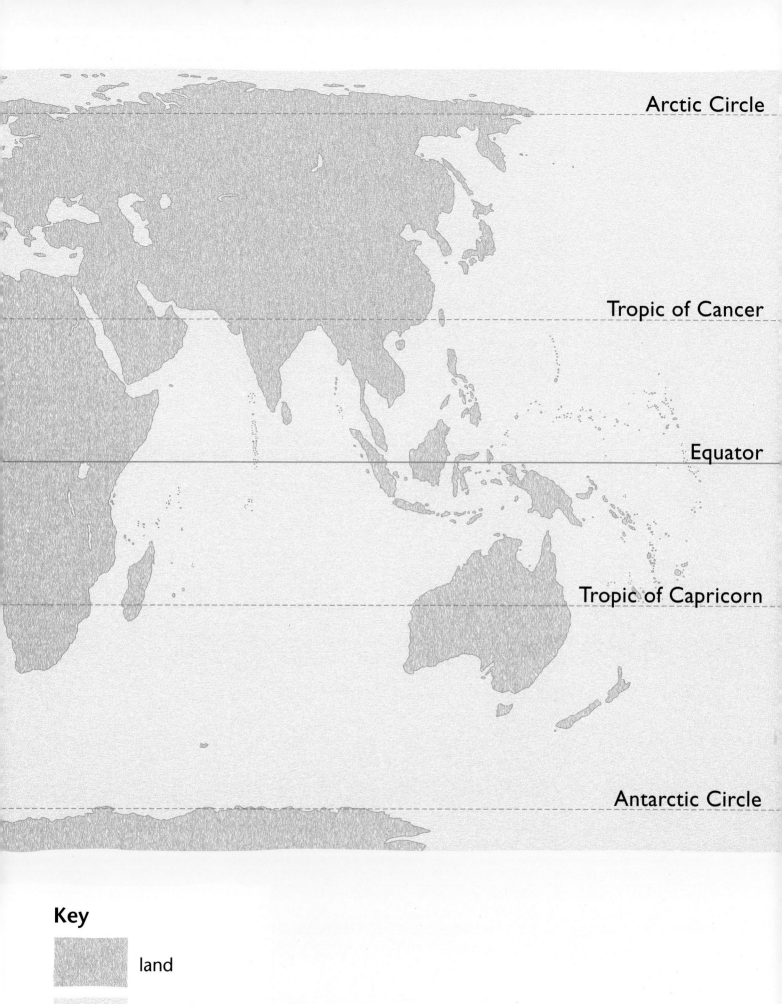

Arctic Circle

Tropic of Cancer

Equator

Tropic of Capricorn

Antarctic Circle

Key

land

sea

The World

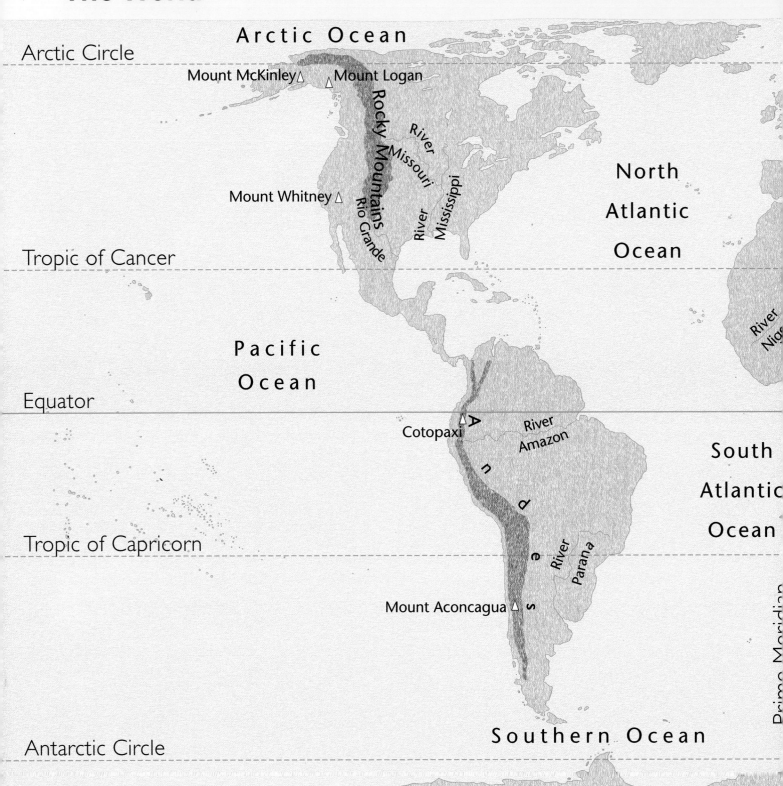

Arctic Circle

Arctic Ocean

Mount McKinley△ △ Mount Logan

Rocky Mountains

River Missouri

River Mississippi

Mount Whitney △

Rio Grande

North Atlantic Ocean

Tropic of Cancer

River Niger

Pacific Ocean

Equator

Cotopaxi △ A

River Amazon

South Atlantic Ocean

n

River Parana

d

Tropic of Capricorn

e

Mount Aconcagua △ s

Prime Meridian

Southern Ocean

Antarctic Circle

14   There are rivers and mountains.

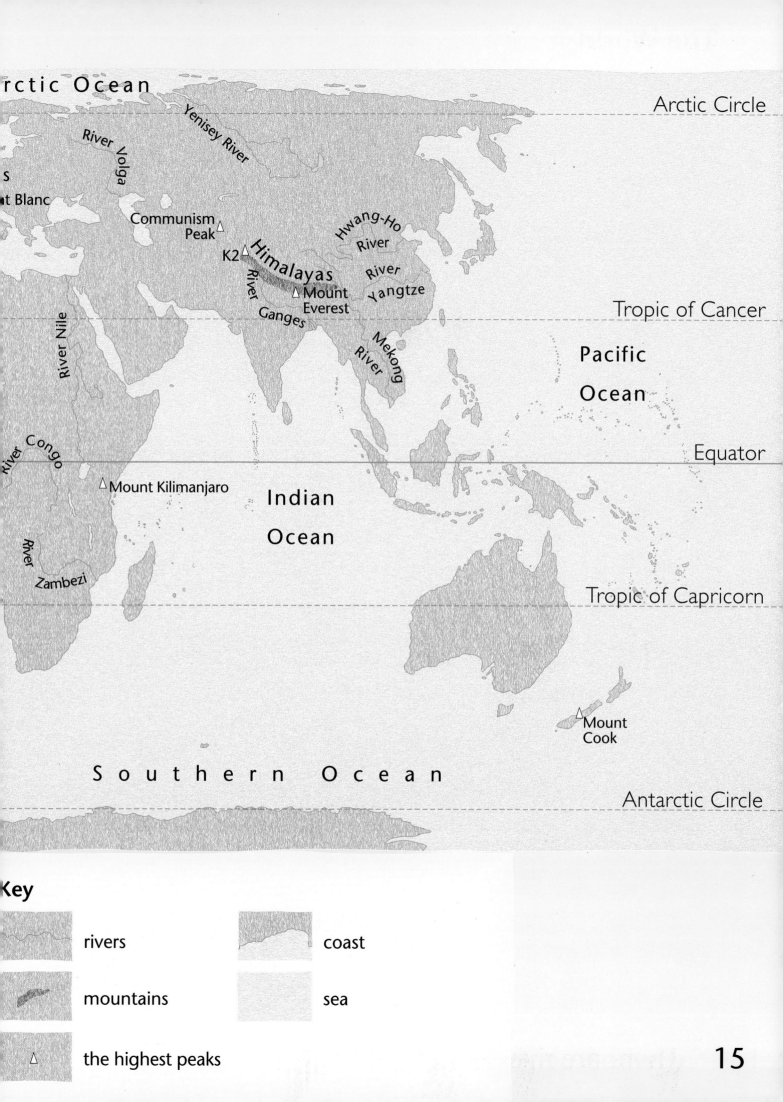

rctic Ocean

Arctic Circle

Yenisey River

River Volga

t Blanc

Communism Peak △

K2 △

Himalayas

Hwang-Ho River

River

River

Yangtze

△ Mount Everest

River Ganges

Mekong River

Tropic of Cancer

River Nile

Pacific

Ocean

River Congo

Equator

△ Mount Kilimanjaro

Indian

Ocean

River Zambezi

Tropic of Capricorn

Southern Ocean

△ Mount Cook

Antarctic Circle

Key

rivers

coast

mountains

sea

△ the highest peaks

The World

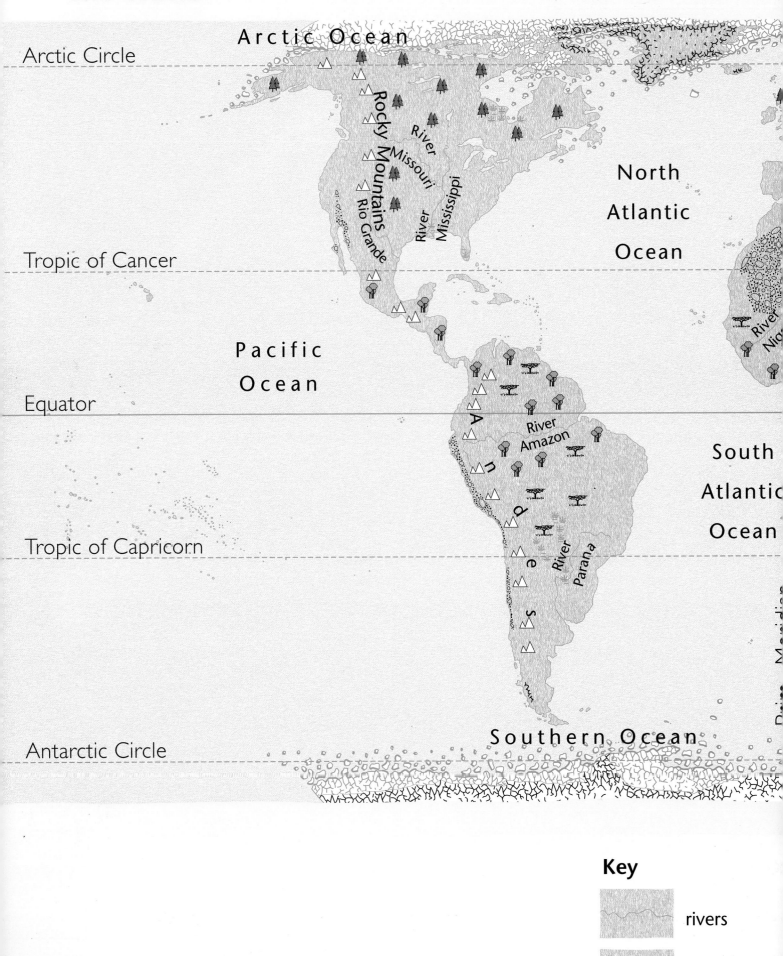

Arctic Circle

Arctic Ocean

Rocky Mountains

River Missouri

Rio Grande

River Mississippi

North Atlantic Ocean

Tropic of Cancer

Pacific Ocean

River Niger

Equator

A n d e s

River Amazon

River Paraná

South Atlantic Ocean

Tropic of Capricorn

Prime Meridian

Southern Ocean

Antarctic Circle

Key

rivers

mountains

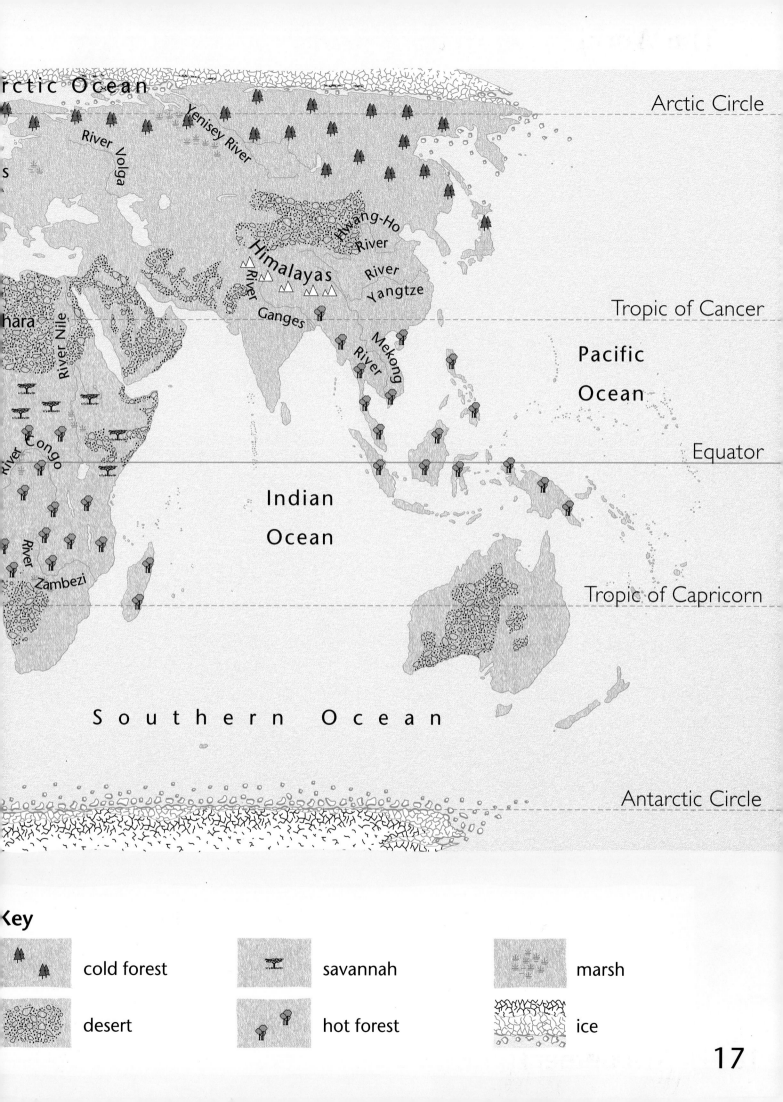

Arctic Ocean

Arctic Circle

River Volga

Yenisey River

Hwang-Ho River

Himalayas

River Ganges

River Yangtze

Mekong River

Tropic of Cancer

Pacific Ocean

hara

River Nile

River Congo

Equator

Indian Ocean

River Zambezi

Tropic of Capricorn

S o u t h e r n   O c e a n

Antarctic Circle

Key

	cold forest		savannah		marsh
	desert		hot forest		ice

17

The World

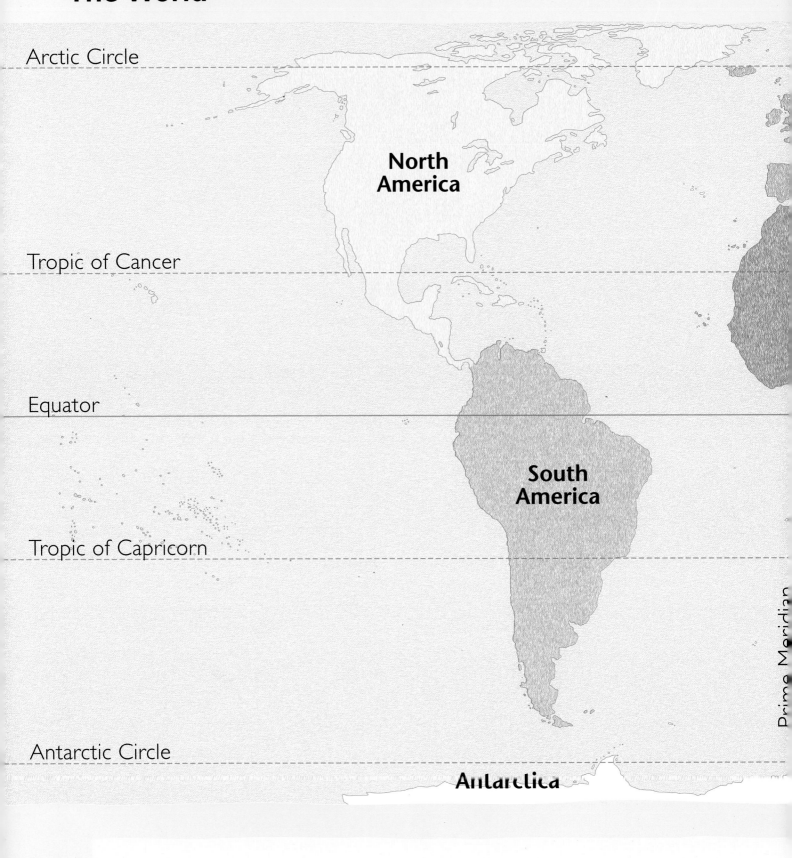

Arctic Circle

North America

Tropic of Cancer

Equator

South America

Tropic of Capricorn

Prime Meridian

Antarctic Circle

Antarctica

Key

These colours are used to show where one continent ends and another begins.

18   There are 7 continents.

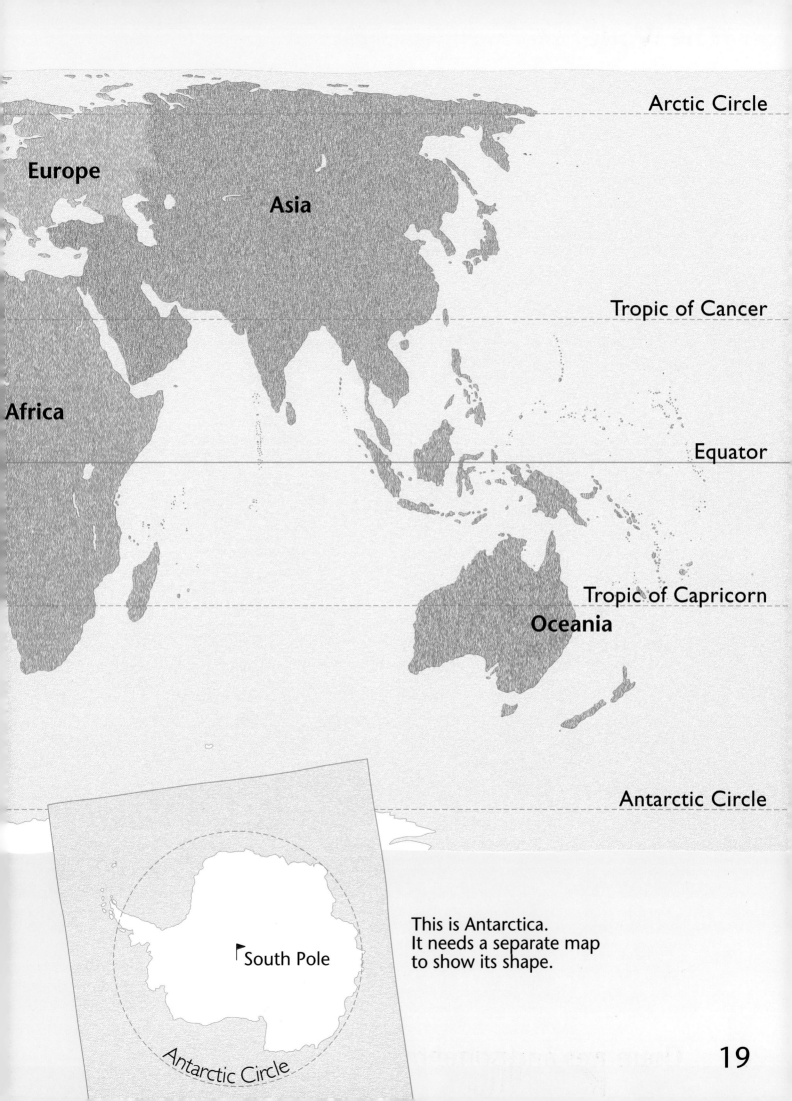

Arctic Circle

Europe

Asia

Tropic of Cancer

Africa

Equator

Tropic of Capricorn

Oceania

Antarctic Circle

South Pole

This is Antarctica.
It needs a separate map
to show its shape.

Antarctic Circle

The World

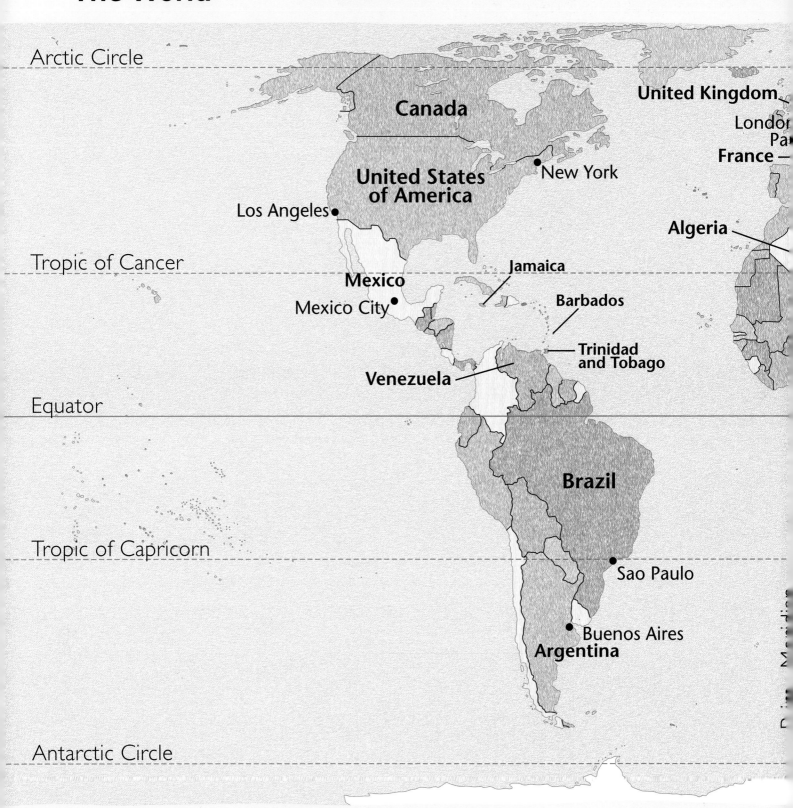

Arctic Circle

Canada

United Kingdom

London

Pa

France

United States
of America

New York

Los Angeles

Algeria

Tropic of Cancer

Mexico

Jamaica

Barbados

Mexico City

Trinidad
and Tobago

Venezuela

Equator

Brazil

Tropic of Capricorn

Sao Paulo

Buenos Aires

Argentina

Antarctic Circle

20   Countries and some major cities.

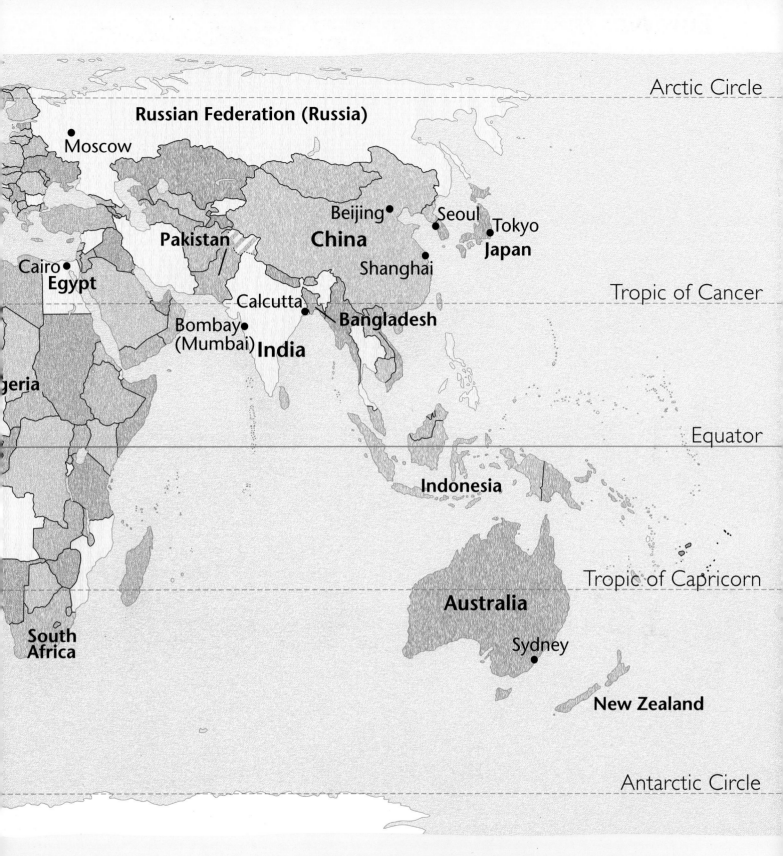

Arctic Circle

Russian Federation (Russia)

• Moscow

Beijing •

China

Seoul

Tokyo

Pakistan

Japan

Cairo •

Shanghai

Tropic of Cancer

Egypt

Calcutta

Bombay •

Bangladesh

geria

(Mumbai) **India**

Equator

Indonesia

Tropic of Capricorn

Australia

South
Africa

Sydney •

New Zealand

Antarctic Circle

ey

These colours are used to show where one country ends and another begins. Some countries are named on the map.

   major cities

Europe

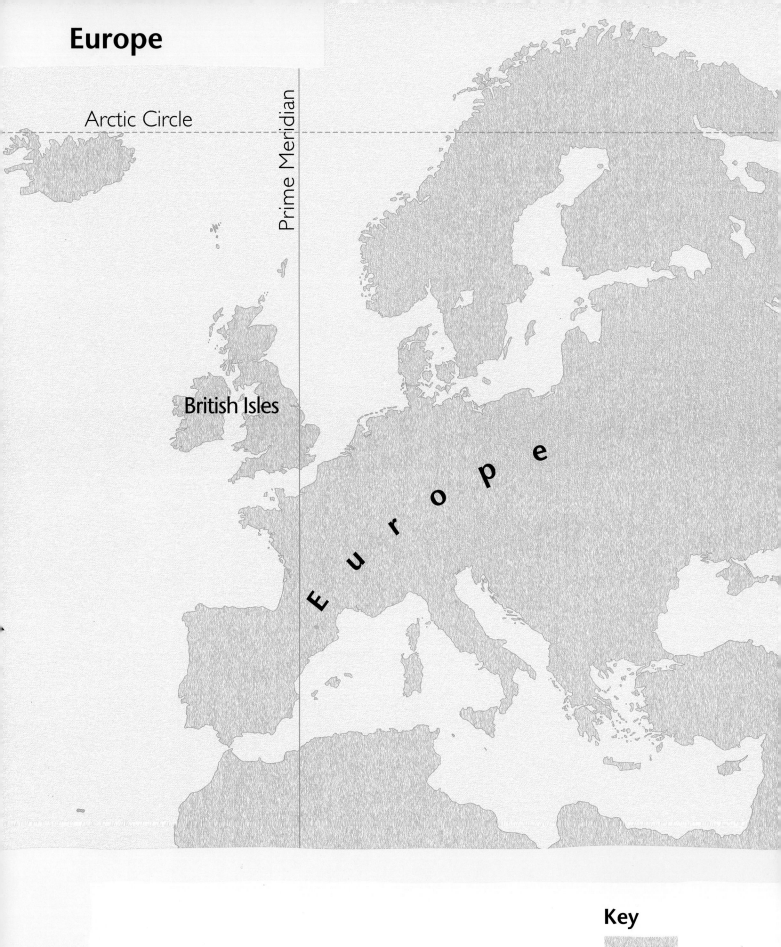

Arctic Circle

Prime Meridian

British Isles

Europe

Key

land

sea

Europe is the smallest continent.

Europe

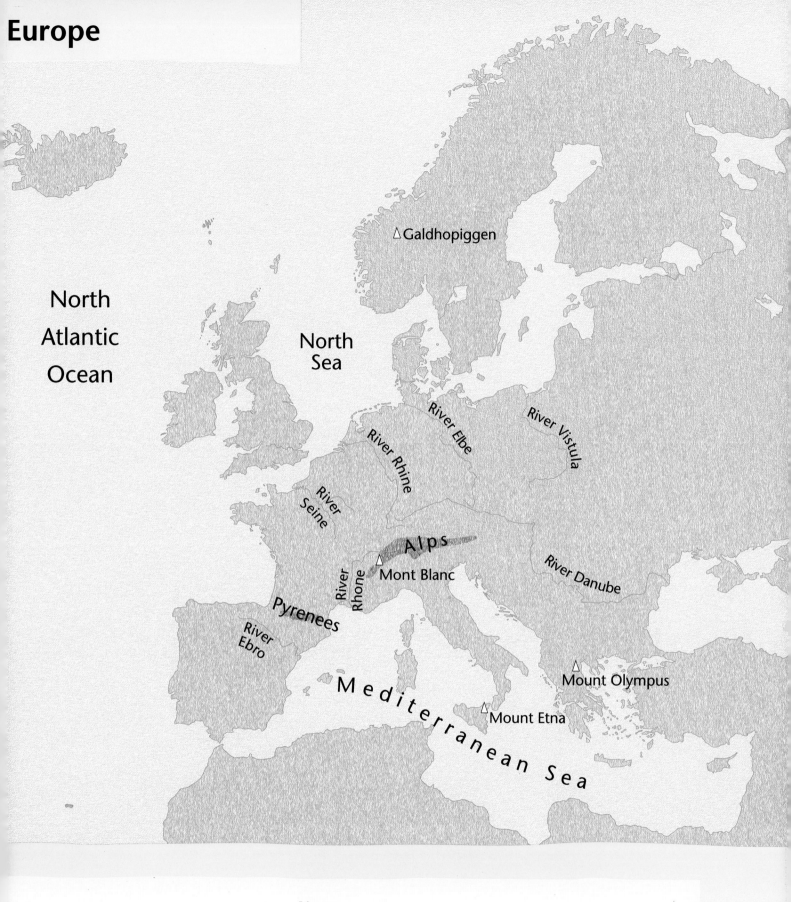

North
Atlantic
Ocean

North
Sea

△ Galdhopiggen

River Elbe

River Vistula

River Rhine

River
Seine

Alps

River
Rhone

△
Mont Blanc

River Danube

Pyrenees

River
Ebro

△ Mount Olympus

△ Mount Etna

M e d i t e r r a n e a n   S e a

Key

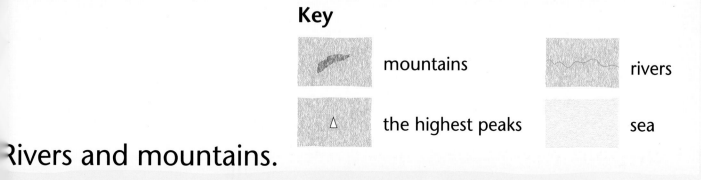

mountains

rivers

△ the highest peaks

sea

Rivers and mountains.

Europe

Iceland

Norway

Sweden

Finland

Estonia

Russian Federation (Russia)

Latvia

Lithuania

Denmark

United Kingdom

Republic of Ireland

Netherlands

Poland

Belarus

Germany

Belgium

Czech Republic

Ukraine

Luxembourg

Liechtenstein

Slovakia

Switzerland

Austria

Hungary

Moldova

France

Slovenia

Croatia

Romania

Monaco

Yugoslavia

San Marino

Bosnia-Herzegovina

Bulgaria

Andorra

Italy

FYRO Macedonia

Portugal

Spain

Albania

Turkey

Greece

Malta

Cyprus

Key

These colours are used to show where one country ends and another begins.

Europe

European Union

Austria

Belgium

Denmark

Finland

France

Germany

Greece

Italy

Luxembourg

Netherlands

Portugal

Republic of Ireland

Spain

Sweden

United Kingdom

Sweden

Finland

Helsinki

Stockholm

Denmark

Copenhagen

United Kingdom

Dublin

Netherlands

Amsterdam

Berlin

London

Germany

Republic of Ireland

Belgium

Brussels

Luxembourg

Luxembourg

Paris

Vienna

France

Austria

Spain

Italy

Rome

Madrid

Lisbon

Greece

Athens

Portugal

Key

Countries that are members of the European Union

■ capital cities

The European Union.

26   This is a picture from a satellite in space.

The British Isles

Key

land

sea

Shetland Islands

Orkney Islands

Lewis

Skye

North Atlantic Ocean

Prime Meridian

North Sea

Isle of Man

Irish Sea

Anglesey

Ireland

Great Britain

North Atlantic Ocean

Isle of Wight

English Channel

Channel Islands

Scale

0   100 km

There are 2 large islands and many small ones.

The British Isles

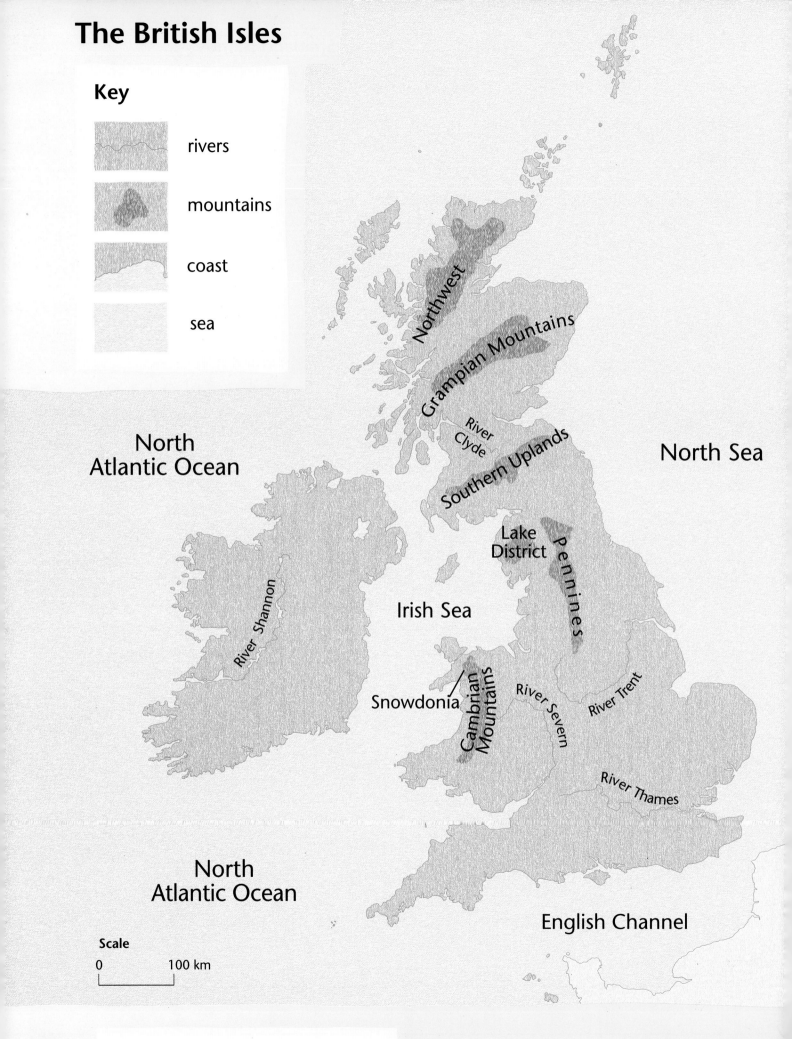

Key

rivers

mountains

coast

sea

North
Atlantic Ocean

North Sea

Northwest

Grampian Mountains

River Clyde

Southern Uplands

Lake District

Pennines

Irish Sea

River Shannon

Snowdonia

Cambrian Mountains

River Severn

River Trent

River Thames

North
Atlantic Ocean

English Channel

Scale

0   100 km

28   Rivers and mountains.

The British Isles

Key

- **■** capital cities

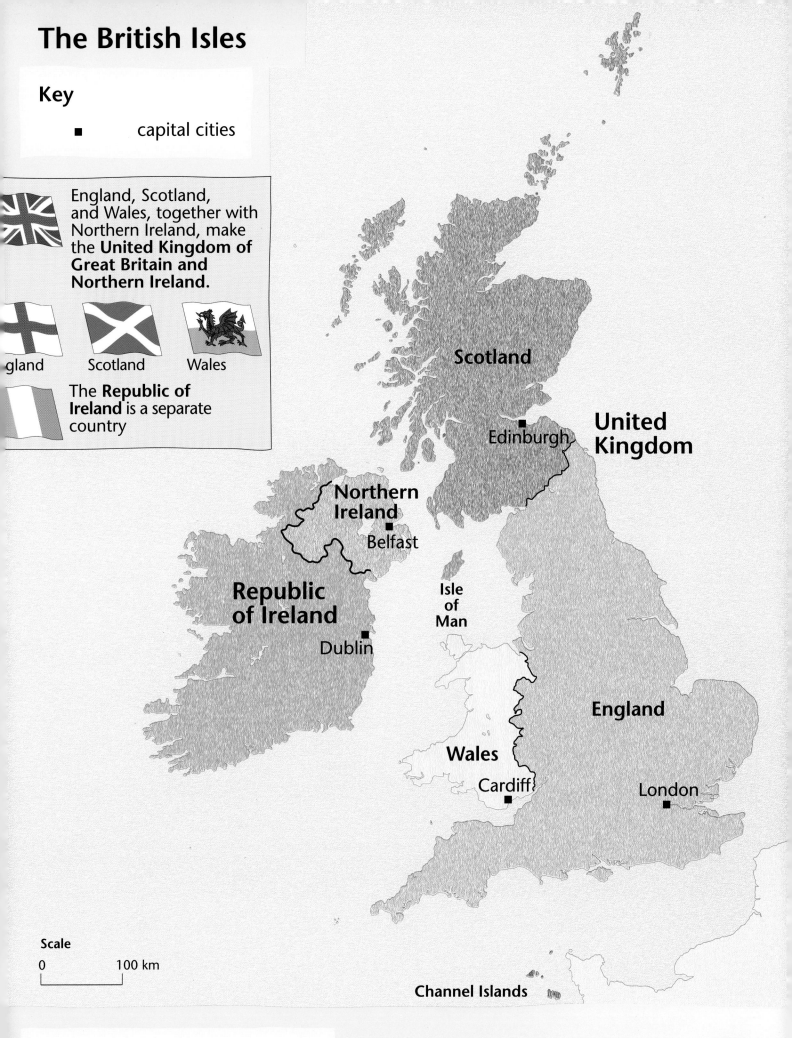

England, Scotland, and Wales, together with Northern Ireland, make the **United Kingdom of Great Britain and Northern Ireland.**

gland　　Scotland　　Wales

The **Republic of Ireland** is a separate country

Scotland

United Kingdom

Edinburgh ■

Northern Ireland

Belfast ■

Republic of Ireland

Dublin ■

Isle of Man

England

Wales

Cardiff ■

London ■

Scale

0　　100 km

Channel Islands

Countries and capitals.

29

The British Isles

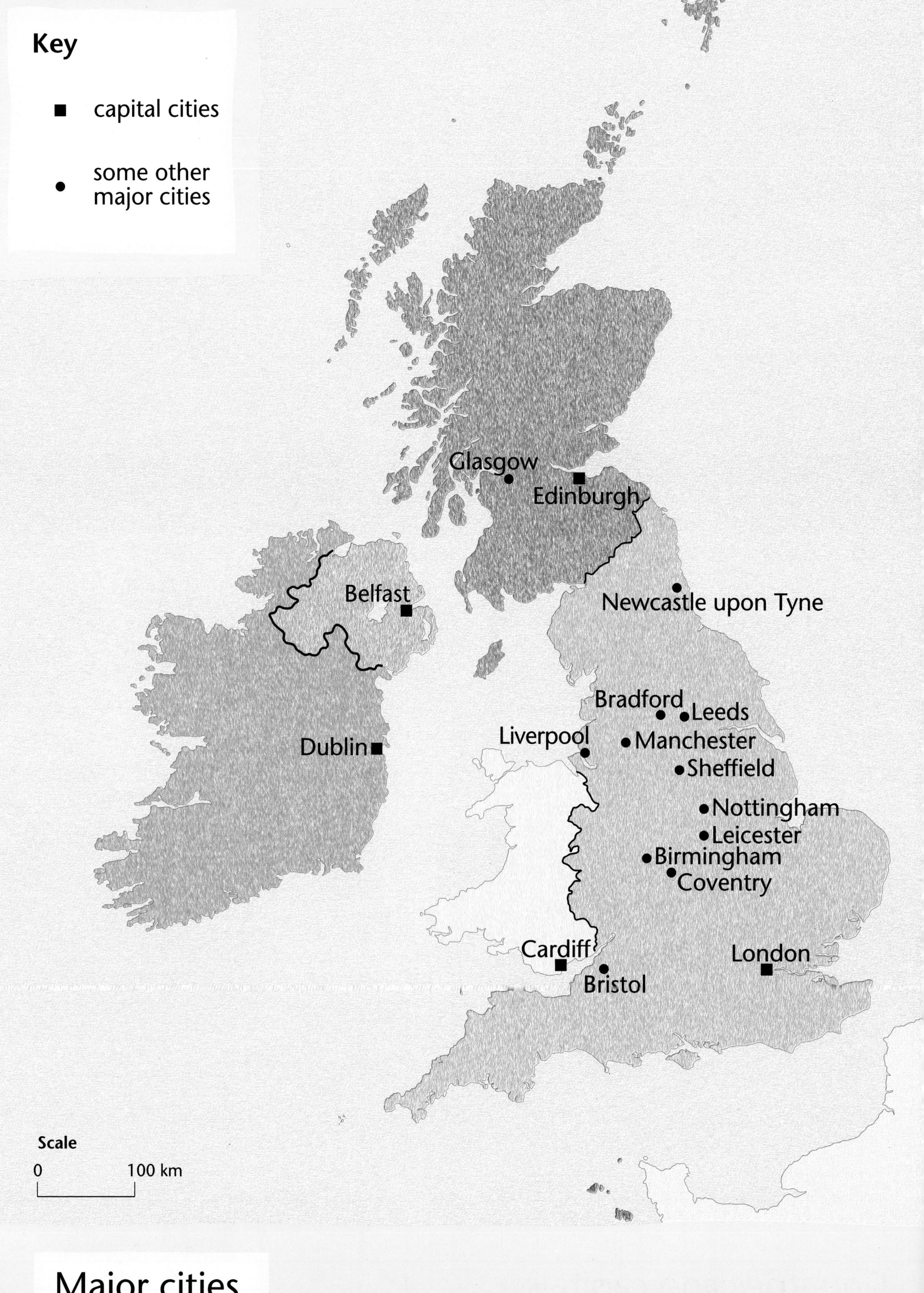

Key
capital cities
some other major cities
Glasgow
Edinburgh
Belfast
Newcastle upon Tyne
Bradford
Leeds
Liverpool
Manchester
Dublin
Sheffield
Nottingham
Leicester
Birmingham
Coventry
Cardiff
London
Bristol
Scale
0
100 km

Major cities.

The British Isles

Key

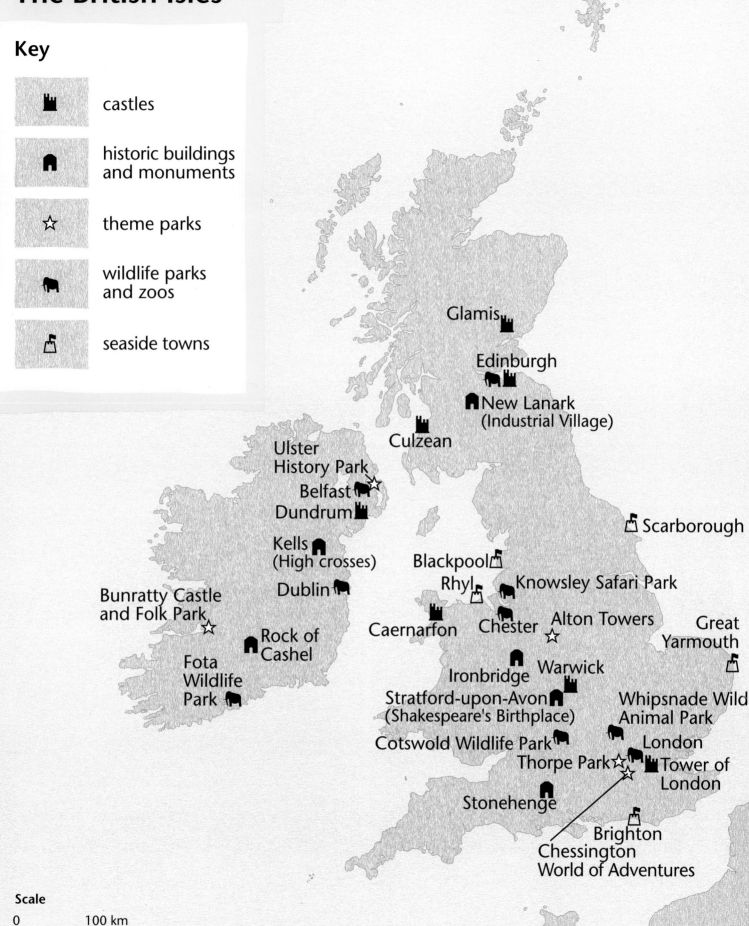

- 🏰 castles
- 🏠 historic buildings and monuments
- ☆ theme parks
- 🐘 wildlife parks and zoos
- 🏰 seaside towns

Glamis

Edinburgh

New Lanark (Industrial Village)

Culzean

Ulster History Park

Belfast

Dundrum

Kells (High crosses)

Scarborough

Blackpool

Rhyl

Knowsley Safari Park

Dublin

Bunratty Castle and Folk Park

Caernarfon

Chester

Alton Towers

Great Yarmouth

Rock of Cashel

Fota Wildlife Park

Ironbridge

Warwick

Stratford-upon-Avon (Shakespeare's Birthplace)

Whipsnade Wild Animal Park

Cotswold Wildlife Park

London

Thorpe Park

Tower of London

Stonehenge

Brighton

Chessington World of Adventures

Scale

0   100 km

Some places to visit.

Index

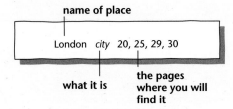

name of place

London *city* 20, 25, 29, 30

what it is

the pages where you will find it

A list of the place names in this atlas.